Correspondence Relative To Dr. Hayman's Expulsion Of P. O. Westfeldt, Of New York, From Rugby School, In March, 1871

J. Beck Publisher

In the interest of creating a more extensive selection of rare historical book reprints, we have chosen to reproduce this title even though it may possibly have occasional imperfections such as missing and blurred pages, missing text, poor pictures, markings, dark backgrounds and other reproduction issues beyond our control. Because this work is culturally important, we have made it available as a part of our commitment to protecting, preserving and promoting the world's literature. Thank you for your understanding.

CORRESPONDENCE

RELATIVE TO

THE REV. DR. HAYMAN'S

EXPULSION OF P. O. WESTFELDT,

OF NEW YORK,

FROM

RUGBY SCHOOL,

IN MARCH, 1871.

Leamington:
PRINTED BY J. BECK, "ADVERTISER" OFFICE, No. 8, UPPER PARADE.

iii.

Mr. Westfeldt, of New York, some years ago placed his three sons at Rugby School; they were all in the School House—the Boarding House kept by the Head Master—and, till recently, he and his sons have been most warmly attached to the School. He has given the name of "Rugby" to a beautiful estate he has in North Carolina. His eldest son was for some time in the Sixth Form, and left at Christmas, 1870. His second son, P. O. Westfeldt, was in March, 1871, in the Form next below the Sixth, eagerly looking forward to the justly coveted honor of joining that Form after Easter, and of being promoted to the School Eleven in the Cricket Field, when he was suddenly, and summarily expelled. He was eighteen years old last winter.

The circumstances of his expulsion are stated in Mr. Field's letter, of the 13th of March, to Dr. Hayman (see post page 7). The statements of that letter were carefully taken from P. O. Westfeldt's mouth. Their accuracy, with two exceptions, is admitted by Dr. Hayman's reply. An appeal was made, on his behalf, to the Trustees of the School, who, after an enquiry at which Dr. Hayman and some of the Sixth Form boys attended, but at which neither Mr. Westfeldt nor his son were present, nor in any way represented, admitted there was some "misunderstanding" and something "to complain of," but took no steps, either to redress the complaint, or clear up the misunderstanding.

Mr. Westfeldt has, therefore, been advised to submit the correspondence to his Son's School-fellows and the Public—confident that Englishmen generally will pronounce a fairer judgment than those have done to whose care the English nation has committed this great school, and on whom he, as a Foreigner, had the strongest claims for justice.

M. Vecqueray is the French and German Master at Rugby School. He also keeps a school to prepare boys for Rugby. All the three Westfeldts were in his house before entering Rugby School. This, it is supposed, is the ground on which he was urged by Dr. Hayman to assume the powers of a Parent towards P. O. Westfeldt, and to remove him on his Father's behalf, though the Atlantic Telegraph placed the Father himself within easy reach.

iv.

The reports which his Father received of P. O. Westfeldt's conduct and progress had been uniformly good and satisfactory, till he received Dr. Hayman's letter of the 2nd of March, stating his son had been removed on his own behalf. This letter, instead of explaining his exact offence, was couched in terms that seemed to describe a hardened and abandoned character,—"by God's help," not quite without "hope,"—and caused Mr. Westfeldt as much surprise as pain, for he was convinced his Son had not deserved expulsion, and felt that he ought to have been consulted before anyone assumed authority to remove him.

It is clear, in fact, that P. O. Westfeldt never was removed by M. Vecqueray, and it would appear that Dr. Hayman repeatedly urged his removal, and ultimately alleged that he was so removed, only because he knew there was no sufficient ground to justify expulsion. M. Vecqueray, in a letter to Mr. Field, dated 21st March, fully explained his part in the matter. Of this letter Dr. Hayman has not allowed M. Vecqueray to permit the publication.—See M. Vecqueray's letter of 22nd May. The want of this permission is much to be regretted; it seems capable only of one explanation.

The Rugby School System of maintaining order by means of the Sixth Form, no doubt, supplies a valuable power to a Master capable of keeping it under proper control ; but if this power be unchecked, it is certain to produce injustice and disorder between those of the Sixth Form and those immediately below—almost their equals. During the time of Arnold, Goulbourn, Tait, and Temple, the scales were so justly balanced that a dispute or misunderstanding is scarcely on record. How far Dr. Hayman endeavours to tread in their footsteps the following instance may help to answer. A boy was lately brought before Dr. Hayman, who said, " You are reported for laughing at prayers." The boy answered, " The Sixth Fellow made a mistake, sir, I did not laugh at prayers." Dr. Hayman replied, "I did not say you laughed at prayers ; I said you were reported for laughing at prayers, and you will do 100 lines."

It is very probable P. O. Westfeldt may have been troublesome to the boys of the Sixth Form in the School House ; but the public is invited to judge, from the following correspondence, how far the Head Master, under whose care and protection he was placed, has discharged the duties he owed to him, and to his Father who was three thousand miles away.

A. S. FIELD.

LEAMINGTON,
1st June, 1871.

CORRESPONDENCE.

School House, Rugby, England,
March 2, 1871.

Dear Sir,

It is with very great reluctance that I write to you, since I have to announce that I have found myself unable to retain your son, P. O. Westfeldt, as a Member of this House.

2nd March, 1871.
Dr. Hayman to Mr. Westfeldt.

It is ten days or more ago that he used language of insolent insubordination to one of the Sixth Form in the House, when engaged in the duty of maintaining its discipline.

This was, however, by the intervention of his Tutor, smoothed over, and on his apologising was condoned. But more lately, viz., on Monday evening last, he was reported to me for again using insolent language, not without a tinge of profaneness, to another Member of the Sixth Form in the House, when similarly engaged in the maintenance of its discipline.

This was followed by, and I think was in no small degree (though I will not say was designedly) the cause of an outbreak of insubordination on the part of the boys lower in the School, which for the time almost subverted discipline (a). There is, indeed, little actual power left to the Sixth Form of maintaining that order with which they are charged, if the boys who are next below the Sixth do not set a good example.

(a) The outbreak here referred to is that of the Monday evening. Two offences only are alleged against P. O. Westfeldt, one on the Monday evening, the other ten days previously. As to the first in date, see Mr. Westfeldt's remarks post page 24.

I was, therefore, compelled to regard his longer continuance in the School House, as inconsistent with that discipline, without which no House can go on. I was, however, anxious to save him from the stigma of expulsion, and I now regard him as removed, in your interest and with your consent presumed, by the friendly intervention of my colleague, M. Vecqueray, from Rugby School, without that stigma (*a*).

I should add, that by Rule, no boy, below the Sixth, can claim to stay after he is 18, and that your son was 18 last Term. His return after the last Holidays was a special indulgence (*b*) which should have enlisted his loyal support of order and discipline. This he certainly has not shown, though, I hope, he has some good qualities, which will, by God's help, enable him to be a good son to you in the future (*c*). In illustration of this, I am bound to add that his feeling on your account was most poignant when I announced my resolution to him.

It gives me the greatest pain to make this communication.

I remain, dear Sir,
Very faithfully yours,
HENRY HAYMAN.

G. G. Westfeldt, Esq.,
New York

(*a*) When expelled from the School House, P. O. Westfeldt was sent to M. Vecqueray's. While there, he was required not to speak to any of his old Schoolfellows—even when accidentally met in the streets. If removed on behalf of his Father, who had the right to impose such a restraint?

(*b*) This is not so. The Rule is simply that at the end of each term, boys who are below certain forms specified for their ages, *may* be told not to return. If not so warned, when received back, their status is, in all respects, the same as if not superannuated.

(*c*) See Note to Page 25, as to the alarming tone of this sentence.

The above letter was received by Mr. Westfeldt, in New York, on about the 18th March, and on the 21st March he telegraphed to Dr. Hayman as follows:— "I can't see the fairness of what has been done. Let Minor (a) prepare to return home at Easter."

18th March, 1871. Mr. Westfeldt to Dr. Hayman.

Blackdown Hill, Leamington,
13th March, 1871.

Dear Sir,

P. O. R. Westfeldt, who has just been dismissed from Rugby School, is staying with me. I have the pleasure of knowing his parents. He and his two brothers have been schoolfellows at Rugby of my three sons, and they are all great friends. His parents are 3,000 miles away; he has no relations nor connections in England. I think he is suffering a great injustice, and I, therefore, feel called upon to make that appeal to you, which I should make if he were my own son, and which I think his Father, if he were here, and in fact every father, would make.

13th March, 1871. Mr. Field to Dr. Hayman.

After careful enquiry, I understand the facts to be these:—A great row lately took place in the School House. The Sixth Form Boys immediately interfered to repress it. Westfeldt was not in the remotest degree connected with it—not even a spectator—but when the Sixth Form Boys came up, he was getting some clothes from his box in the passage. Mr. Goldsmidt (b) (who for

---

(a) Minor, means the youngest Westfeldt, who however was never informed of this telegram. The cruelty of withholding this telegram from the two brothers seems inexplicable.

(b) Goldsmidt is one of the Sixth Form in the School House.

some time had not been on friendly terms with him) said to him, "Did you throw that slipper at me?" Westfeldt said, "Do you think I should be at the trouble to throw a slipper at you?" Mr. Goldsmidt said, "It is a plain question and I require a plain answer." Westfeldt said, "I should not condescend to throw a slipper at such a fool as you."

I can scarcely believe this to be the whole, or the correct statement of the case. If I am misinformed, you will no doubt kindly put me right. But I am assured this was the whole of Westfeldt's offence, and that the facts I have stated are not disputed; except, I believe, it has been asserted that Westfeldt swore at Mr. Goldsmidt. But Westfeldt denies that he did so. I have seen a boy who was present, who also denies it. I do not think Westfeldt is in the habit of swearing, and, in my own mind I fully acquit him of this aggravation.

Considering the importance of upholding the authority of the Sixth Form, I do not for a moment deny that Westfeldt was guilty of an offence, which required notice and punishment. But, as the Father of a boy now in the School, and who has had sons there the last ten years, I feel bound to say I think the offence wholly insufficient to justify expulsion; and that if I had understood Rugby boys were liable to expulsion on such grounds, I should have hesitated to send my sons there, and that (inconvenient as it is to change a school, and much as I should regret my son leaving Rugby) I must hesitate to keep him there, for no boy below the Sixth Form can, in such circumstances, be safe.

But this is far from the whole of Westfeldt's grievance. Mr. Goldsmidt brought the matter before you as

Head Master. You enquired into the case, and sat in judgment upon it. And your decision was, that Westfeldt should make a public apology in Hall, and a private apology to Goldsmidt, and should write out 2,000 lines. This sentence was at once submitted to; the public and the private apologies were both made, a large part of the lines were done, and the rest were in progress, when Westfeldt was ordered to leave the School.

No new offence was in the meantime committed—nor even alleged to have been committed—and the only grounds I can learn for this further most severe and dreadful punishment, blasting Westfeldt's future fair name and reputation, are that he is said to have smiled or sneered while making his apology, and to have been guilty of some old offences to the Sixth Form, long forgotten, but now again raked up.

Fortunately for my young friend, you were, as he tells me, yourself present at both apologies, and at the time pronounced them both sufficient, and said that you hoped the matter would no more be heard of.

I have always understood, one of the first principles of justice is, that no one should be twice tried, or twice punished for the same offence; and Westfeldt having faithfully carried out your own sentence, the matter should, I think, in your own words, there have ended.

With great confidence in your sense of justice, I, therefore, appeal to you to carry out your own first judgment—a judgment which I feel sure all parents of boys, and public opinion (if ever called upon to consider it) will say abundantly punished the offence committed.

Under the circumstances stated, I feel sure you will excuse me for interfering in a matter, with which, some may think, I have nothing to do. I assure you it gives me the deepest pain to do so, as I have hitherto looked back upon my own, and my sons' connection with Rugby School, with the most lively and sincere feelings of satisfaction and gratitude.

If you should think an interview desirable, I will call upon you at any time you will appoint, but if on Wednesday not before Three o'clock p.m.

I remain, dear Sir,
Your very obedient and faithful servant,
A. S. FIELD.

The Rev. Dr. Hayman,
Rugby.

Rugby, March 14th, 1871.

Dear Sir,

14th March, 1871. Dr. Hayman to Mr. Field.

I must be allowed to correct you on a most important point. Westfeldt is not expelled. I view him as removed from the School by an arrangement made on his Father's behalf. It is not uncommon for such arrangements to be made, in cases where a boy's stay is inconsistent with discipline, and where it is not intended to cast upon him the stigma of expulsion.

I should add that, in the case of a boy superannuated as Westfeldt was by School Rule in the previous term, such boy is allowed to return only on sufferance, and under the distinct understanding that his conduct is to be in support of authority. If he becomes insubordinate, he is liable to be told, "You are here on good behaviour, and you must now withdraw." (a)

I really cannot go into the details of a case which I have most anxiously considered in every stage, with a view expressly of considering if it were possible to reconcile Westfeldt's return with the interests of discipline. I have, after that full consideration, come to the conclusion that it cannot be so reconciled, and, deprecating every imputation of personal discourtesy, I must be allowed to say that there the case must rest, although I cannot admit your information concerning the facts as adequate. I have, of course, written fully to Mr. Westfeldt on the subject, and remain

Very faithfully yours,
HENRY HAYMAN.

A. S. Field, Esq.

Blackdown Hill, Leamington,
16th March, 1871.

Dear Sir,

I have duly received your letter of the 14th inst., for which I am obliged.

16th March, 1871. Mr. Field to Dr. Hayman.

Under the circumstances stated in my former letter, I thought I had a right, and was indeed called upon, to write you on Westfeldt's behalf, and I was so advised by several friends of good judgment and experience; but, as your letter insists that explanations are due from

---

(a) See Note to Page 6 ante. It would be well for parents clearly to understand whether the power here claimed does belong to the Head-Master of Rugby School. The printed Rules sent to parents do not say so.

you to his Father alone, I will not, for the present at least, question that position.

Two explanations, however, your letter gives me. But from the information I have received, I am still compelled to believe Westfeldt was expelled from the School House; and with regard to his superannuation, that was no new circumstance arising after you had first judged his case, and he had carried out your judgment.

In conclusion, I am bound to say, at present, it seems plain to me Westfeldt is suffering a great injustice, and I deeply regret my former letter has not induced you to remove it, either by recalling him to the School House, or by arranging for his entrance into Mr. Vecqueray's or some other house, or by some other plan; and if his Father does not bring the matter before a Court of Justice, the Trustees, or the Public (which I fully expect he will do), I shall reserve to myself the liberty of appealing to one or both of these last tribunals, if I shall hereafter consider it proper.

I remain
Your very obedient and faithful servant,
A. S. FIELD

Rev. Dr. Hayman.

Leamington, 24th March, 1871.

My Lord,

24th March, 1871. Mr. Field to Lord Leigh, a Trustee of Rugby School.

I take the liberty of sending to you, as a Trustee of Rugby School, a copy of a correspondence between the Head Master and myself. I had intended to take no further step, till I had seen whether Dr. Hayman's letter to Mr.

Westfeldt altered the case; and if not, then to appeal either to the Trustees, or to the Public, or to both, as might seem best. But hearing a meeting of Trustees is to be held to-morrow, at which Westfeldt's case may come under consideration, I thought it right at once to beg you to read this correspondence, and to bring it under the notice of the meeting. I cannot, I think, be blamed for doing this before I have seen all Dr. Hayman's explanations, because he can give them direct to the Trustees. I may, however, say two telegrams have been received from Mr. Westfeldt, who is dissatisfied with Dr. Hayman's explanations to him. Dr. Hayman in his letter to me says, he corrects my statement in two particulars. I feel sure my statement is substantially correct throughout, and can be proved to be so, and I think his letter must be assumed to admit its accuracy in other respects.

As to the first correction—I am so positively assured that Westfeldt was not removed by any arrangement made on his father's behalf, that, grave and serious as the question is, I venture to say I am confident that Dr. Hayman's assertion is untrue—and if untrue, he must know it is untrue. If, therefore, the Trustees enter into this painful case, I trust they will enquire, with care and determination, into its truth.

On the second point—it is true that Westfeldt was superannuated, but he was so when Dr. Hayman judged his case, and awarded punishment. It was no new circumstance, afterwards arising, and could not therefore justify a reopening of the case

The School House, fallen from its high position, when 14 or 15 of the best boys of the Sixth Form were there, has now only 2 or 3, and those not of the best—at all events in the estimation of their fellows. Two of these are personal enemies of Westfeldt. Boys, even of the Sixth Form at Rugby, are still boys, and if thought by their Schoolfellows unworthy of respect, I apprehend those Schoolfellows, ipso facto, are not to be expelled—especially after the Head Master has judged their want of respect, and has awarded a different punishment.

Should the Trustees be able, and think it right to enter into this case, I shall not, of course, send the correspondence to the Public Papers, if you desire me not to do so. If otherwise, it is my present intention to appeal to public opinion.

I remain, my Lord,

Your very obedient and faithful servant,

A. S. FIELD.

The Right Hon. Lord Leigh.

Blackdown Hill, Leamington,
27th March 1871.

My Lord,

27th March, 1871.
Mr. Field to Lord Leigh.

I am extremely obliged to you for laying before the Trustees of Rugby School my correspondence with Dr. Hayman on Westfeldt's expulsion.

I am deeply interested in the subject, not only from my friendship with Westfeldt, and his family, and from his lonely position here, his Father being in America, but also because I have a son in the School House, and 1 consider him no longer safe there, and I shall remove him at Easter—earlier than I had intended.

I am, therefore, much grieved that you may not be able to attend the adjourned meeting next Thursday. I feel most strongly the interests and prosperity of the School require that the matter should be fully investigated, and therefore I venture to urge your attendance, if your engagements should possibly allow you.

The questions are:—

1st. Whether a saucy word from a Rugby boy to one of the Sixth Form, who was his personal enemy, justifies expulsion.

2nd. Whether, when the Headmaster has held a formal and serious enquiry into such an offence, and has awarded a different punishment, which the offender has suffered, he may still be expelled without having committed any new offence.

3rd. That in defending the steps he has taken, the Headmaster has written that Westfeldt was not expelled, but was removed by arrangement on his Father's behalf and this statement I am bound positively to assert is untrue, and if investigated, I am convinced its untruth will be made clear.

Such grave questions ought in some way to be thoroughly investigated.

> I remain my Lord,
> Your very obedient and faithful servant,
> A. S. FIELD.

The Right Honourable
    Lord Leigh.

Leamington, 27th March, 1871.

Dear Sir,

27th March, 1871. Mr. Field to H. C. Wise, Esq., M.P., a Trustee of Rugby School.

Lord Leigh, at my request, kindly laid before the Trustees of Rugby School, the copy of a correspondence between Dr. Hayman and myself, relative to the expulsion of a boy named Westfeldt. I understand that correspondence will come under the consideration of an adjourned meeting next Thursday, and that Lord Leigh will probably not be there.

If you had been in the country, I should have sought your permission to explain this matter to you personally; but as I find you will not be here, I venture to write to you on the subject. Although I have so slight an acquaintance with you, and that acquaintance has unfortunately arisen rather from points of difference than of agreement, I feel sure you will not on that account, hesitate to give what I have to say, all the consideration it may deserve. I seek from you only such decision upon it, as you may think will best promote the prosperity of Rugby School.

I am deeply interested in the subject, not only from my friendship with Westfeldt, and his family, and from his lonely position here—his Father being in America—but also because I have myself a son in the School House, whom I feel compelled to remove at Easter—sooner than I had intended—because I consider him no longer safe there.

Boys have a keen sense of justice; and in consequence of the treatment Westfeldt has received (which is generally believed to have been forced on the Headmaster by the boys of the Sixth Form against his own better judgement), there is a general feeling of disgust and rebellion through the School House, which has become too hot for the Sixth Form boys; and I hear this morning they are all leaving at Easter, with others besides.

My letter to Dr. Hayman sets out the whole case. His reply, I think, amounts to an admission of all that I have said except on two points, upon which, he says, he corrects me. These are

1st. He says Westfeldt was not expelled, but was removed by arrangement made on his Father's behalf. This statement, however, I am compelled flatly to contradict, and if investigated, I am confident it will be found to be untrue.

2nd. He says Westfeldt was superannuated; but so he was when Dr. Hayman judged his case and awarded punishment. It was no new circumstance, arising afterwards, and could not therefore justify a re-opening of the case.

The questions involved in the case are these—

1st. Whether a saucy word from a Rugby boy to one of the Sixth Form (and who in this case was his personal enemy) justifies expulsion.

2nd. Whether when the Headmaster has held a formal enquiry on such an offence, and has solemnly pronounced a different judgment, which the offender has suffered, he may still be expelled, without having committed any new offence.

3rd. That in his defence the Headmaster has written that Westfeldt was not expelled, but was removed by arrangement, and this statement I am bound positively to assert is untrue.

These questions, it seems to me, are of so grave and serious a character as to require thorough investigation.

I remain,

Your most obedient servant,

A. S. FIELD.

H. C. Wise Esq., M.P.,
6, King's Street, St. James's,
London.

Carlton Club, March 28th, 1871.

Dear Sir,

28th March, 1871.
Mr. Wise to Mr. Field.

I beg to acknowledge the receipt of your letter this morning. No apology I am sure is necessary for writing to me, on this, or any other subject.

In a general way, it is very unusual for the Trustees to interfere in any of the internal arrangements of Rugby School. I mean as far as the acts of the Headmaster are concerned. There may be, however, exceptional cases that ought to be brought under their notice. The case you refer to may, possibly, be one of such a character, and as I see it is put down amongst the Agenda for our meeting on Thursday, no doubt it will receive every attention from the Trustees on that occasion. I am sorry that Lord Leigh will be unavoidably absent on Thursday—so he told me yesterday.

    Believe me, Dear Sir,
      Yours faithfully,
        H. C. WISE.

A. S. Field, Esq.

    Rugby, 13th April, 1871.

Dear Sir,

13th April, 1871. The Clerk to the Trustees to Mr. Field.

I am directed to inform you that the Trustees of Rugby School have considered the statements contained in your letter addressed to Lord Leigh in reference to the case of Mr. Westfeldt, together with statements in reference thereto by members of the Sixth Form, by Mr. Vecqueray, and by the Headmaster, and are of opinion that, upon the whole, there is not much to complain of.

There has evidently been some misunderstanding in the case, but it is clear that it was Dr. Hayman's wish, in the part which he took in the matter, to avoid the actual expulsion of the boy, by arranging for his removal from the school. They consider Westfeldt's conduct towards the Sixth in the School House as very rebellious.

    I am, dear sir,
      Yours faithfully,
       EDMUND HARRIS,
        Clerk to the Trustees.

A. S. Field, Esq.

Leamington, 14th April, 1871.

Dear Sir,

I have received your letter of yesterday, informing me of the conclusion come to by the Trustees of Rugby School in reference to the case of Westfeldt.

I beg to differ from their conclusion, which appears to have been arrived at *ex-parte*.

I remain, dear Sir,

Yours faithfully,

Edmund Harris, Esq. A. S. FIELD.

14th April, 1871. Mr. Field to The Clerk to the Trustees.

New York, 21st March, 1871.

Dear Sir,

I have had the pain to receive your note of the 2nd March, and I have also a letter from each one of my sons.

These three communications have been most earnestly and anxiously contemplated for three days, and the only conclusion I have been able to arrive at yet, is comprised in my Telegram of this date, namely, "I can't see the fairness of what has been done"—to which I added, "Let Minor (a) prepare to return home at Easter."

To be excluded from notice or information (whilst the Telegraph was at your service) before a summary

21st March, 1871. Mr. Westfeldt to Dr. Hayman.

(a) "Minor" means Mr. Westfeldt's third son, who, never having been informed of this telegram, had to cross the Atlantic by himself a week or two after P. O. Westfeldt.

execution of an extremely severe sentence, naturally prompts me to place my children within my reach.

I shall take an early opportunity to submit to you a fuller answer to the note you have favoured me with, and in the meantime, I beg of you to facilitate the return of my younger son. Messrs. C. M. Price, the Temple, Liverpool, will pay the accounts of both my sons, if you will be so good as to send them to them.

I am, very respectfully,

Your obedient servant,

GEO. WESTFELDT.

The Rev. H. Hayman, D.D.

New York, 30th of March, 1871.

Dear Sir,

On 21st of this month, I acknowledged your note of the 2nd, and asked that my younger son might be prepared to return home at Easter.

I now come to place my thoughts before you on the unfairness of the sentence upon my elder son.

I am convinced that he had nothing whatever to do with the "*row*" on the Monday evening you speak of, and that he came from down stairs. I am also sure that he did not throw the slipper at Goldschmidt, and that the words used, and the manner of Goldschmidt implied an accusation which was false; and that gave rise to an

30th March, 1871. Mr. Westfeldt to Dr. Hayman.

impertinent answer, but neither of my sons' reports of the words used, show any profanity.

Under these circumstances, it seems to me, that your reproof, and the atonement made by your order—publicly and privately—were not only sufficient, but final. It could not be just to bring him up, after punishment, for a second sentence—and that one a summary expulsion, without a word of warning to himself, or his parents. I see no cause for your intended infliction of the stigma of expulsion, and it would follow that a compulsory removal, to avoid the stigma, is not based upon justice. Whatever may be the momentary effect of an unjust act, it certainly cannot produce permanent advantage either to Discipline, to the Sixth Form, or to Rugby School. In your position as Head Master, you had to act as judge, or else the *accusers* were permitted to *condemn*, which is very wrong. And you held another position to my son, as inmate of your house. He was entitled to all the protection inseparable from the exercise of delegated parental authority, and it does not appear to me that he received such protection. You say the previous offence was punished and condoned, which I take to mean pardoned, and therefore not punishable again; although I admit that the repetition of an offence should have some weight in deciding upon a new sentence. That my son may have been troublesome to the Sixth Fellows is very possible—but I have reason to believe it quite as possible that they were not free from wrong prejudices, and unfair bias.

My son appears to have been most severely dealt with—for an example—upon insufficient grounds, to strengthen the authority of his accusers. At the same time, you thought it expedient to make another example of my younger son, by flogging him, for sleeping out of his room, and being under suspicions which (so far as I am aware) were not acted upon against others equally liable to them, of participating in the "row" on the Monday evening. I am constrained to say, that this appears to me an outrageous punishment for the offence. I believe the records of both my sons have been fair, for a long time, at Rugby.

I have shared my three boys attachment for Rugby and its excellent school—as we have known it for many years past: and it is very painful to me to feel that the entire confidence, which I took so much pleasure in, has been disturbed.

I am very respectfully,
Your obedient servant,
GEO. WESTFELDT.

The Rev. H. Hayman, D.D.

New York, 14th April, 1871.

Sir,

My son Philip arrived here yesterday, and I am surprised to find that when he left Liverpool, on the 1st of this month, he was ignorant of my instructions for the return of his younger brother at Easter; otherwise, he would have waited for him, and he is confident that his adviser in Liverpool, my good friend Mr. Norman S. Walker, would have approved of his so doing. I have a letter from my younger son, dated 29th March, at

14th April, 1871. Mr. Westfeldt to Dr. Hayman.

which time he also was ignorant of my wishes as telegraphed to you on the 21st of March. I am assured by the operators here that the telegram must have reached you on the 22nd of March, and that proof thereof shall be forthcoming. Permit me to ask why the purport of my telegram was withheld from my sons, aud from friends who, you were aware, interested themselves in their protection? At present I am unable to discover a straightforward purpose in your silence.

After seeing my son Philip, I am more strongly impressed with the injustice done to him. In the matter of the offence with which you commence in your note to me of the 2nd of March, and in regard to which you wrote, "this was, however, by the intervention of his Tutor, smoothed over, and, on his apology, was condoned," the truth now appears to me that there was no smoothing over, no condoning, but a mutual apology exchanged between the two boys, and the conduct of both, in the "making up" was approved by their Tutor, Mr. Scott, to whom my son begs leave to refer.

Such being the case, and not as you stated it to me, that portion of my letter of the 30th of March which referred to your statement becomes unnecessary, and there is no sequence of offence to be considered in your last most unfair sentence upon my son. In my letter of the 30th of March I passed over your final prop for an injustice committed—that my son was 18 last term, and that his return was a special indulgence, which called for special duties, and, if I understand you rightly, these circumstances warrant a new code of justice to be applied, in case he erred afterwards. I did not believe it necessary to point out to the Head Master of Rugby, that the strongest point in such an argument is totally inapplicable to the case in question; and I have reason to believe that it was an afterthought, gathered after the sentence had been decided upon. Neither my son nor I had any intimation whatsoever of any "special indulgence," or its consequences; nor was I, until very lately, aware of the Rule under which my son might have been superannuated. I assure you I should not have sought such "special indulgence" for him, under your protection of him, had I been informed that he remained on unwilling sufferance, or of the Rule. As to previous conduct of my son, which in this case has a right to be considered, I would beg information from the Bishop of Exeter, and from the Tutors of the School House, who know much better about it than I can do. My impression is, from the reports made to me for about five years from the School House, and previously during several years from M. Vecqueray, that his conduct has oftener been marked "good" than anything else, and never "bad" or "indifferent."

It appears to me that you could not have been ignorant of some good in him, when you said to him on the occasion of sentencing him to Public and Private apology for insolence to Goldschmidt, that you regretted having to punish him then, for you had thought of him "As one that you could trust, and give the Sixth Form power to." (a)

My younger sons' report of his punishment, is as follows (after writing of his brother) " I myself was sent

---

(a) The concluding sentence of Dr. Hayman's letter to Mr. Westfeldt (see ante Page 6) seems intended to portray a character almost abandoned—decidedly unfit for Rugby. That he has any good left is mere matter of hope. Yet shortly for on Wednesday night, and Dr. Hayman said it was an unheard of offence that I should sleep in another room than my own, and said he must flog me. I was flogged, but did not mind it a bit for the pain, and disgrace there was none. He said, even if I did not know that it was wrong to sleep out of my room, that it looked as though I had gone to hide there, from some of the Sixth Fellows, and so he must make an example of me." Surely the Sixth Fellows must be unfit for their position, if they require to be upheld by such expedients as were resorted to in my cases.

I enclose copies of my letters of 21st and 30th March and I shall place the whole correspondence before Mr. A. S. Field of Leamington, to use as he thinks proper and to represent me.

I am,
Your obebient servant,
GEO. WESTFELDT.

Rev. H. Hayman, D.D.

Leamington, 8th May, 1871.

Dear Sir,

I enclose you a check &c., &c.

8th May, 1871. Mr. Field to Dr. Hayman.

Mr. Westfeldt, of New York, has sent me your letter to him of the 2nd March, which (in your letter to me) you call a full explanation of the case. It throws no new light on the matter, and is a very lame excuse

---

before his dismissal Dr. Hayman thought of giving him Sixth Form powers, and shortly after told his younger brother to give his "kind regards" to P. O. Westfeldt and desired him not to consider himself disgraced, and told the whole of the School House in their Dining-hall that P. O. Westfeldt was not dismissed.

for his son's expulsion. And to call that expulsion a removal with his Father's consent, is a miserable subterfuge, unsupported by fact.

Mr. Westfeldt is highly indignant at the cruel injustice his son has met with while under your care and protection.

I remain,
Your obedient servant,
Rev. Dr. Hayman. A. S. FIELD.

School House, Rugby,
9th May, 1871.

Dear Sir,

I beg to acknowledge your check for £37 13s. 8d., and remain,

Faithfully yours,
A. S. Field, Esq. HENRY HAYMAN.

9th May, 1871. Dr. Hayman to Mr. Field.

Leamington, 13th May, 1871.

Dear Sir,

I have at last heard from Mr. Westfeldt, who is of course very indignant at the treatment his son has met with at Rugby. He places himself in my hands to set his son right before the world, and to seek that redress from public opinion which he has failed to get from Dr. Hayman.

On the advice of friends, I have determined to publish all letters which have passed on the subject. Of course, I must publish your letter to me of 21st March, informing me you had never taken on yourself the responsi-

13th May, 1871. Mr. Field to Mr. Vecqueray.

bility of removing Philip. Considering your connection with Dr. Hayman, I would have avoided this if it were possible; but it is a most material feature which I cannot omit; and being now expressly authorised by Mr. Westfeldt, I have a right to require an express answer from you, whether you did remove his son or not, and to publish this answer. I trust, therefore, you will agree that I am fully justified in publishing your letter—indeed I hope you may have no objection to my doing so.

I remain, dear Sir,
Yours truly,
A. S. FIELD.

J. Vecqueray, Esq.,
    Hill Brow, Rugby.

Hill Brow, Rugby, May 15, 1871.

Dear Sir,

15th March, 1871. Mr. Vecqueray to Mr. Field.

I much regret the application you have made to me, for permission to print and publish, together with other papers relating to Westfeldt, a letter I wrote to you on the 21st March.

That letter, in answer to your enquiries, only contains such matters of fact as I have since repeated, almost verbatim, before the Trustees of Rugby School. Still I cannot allow you to publish it. As an Assistant Master I cannot possibly consent to my name being used in a public controversy, the object of which is obviously hostile to the Head Master.

I would strongly urge you not to bring this subject into print. I fear that such a public revival of old troubles and grievances would be rather detrimental to the good of Rugby School, than of any service to the interests of Westfeldt.

I remain, dear sir,
Yours truly,
A. S. Field, Esq.   J. W. VECQUERAY.

Leamington, 19th May, 1871.

Dear Sir,

I duly received your last letter, objecting to the publication of your former letter of the 21st March.

19th May, 1871. Mr. Field to Mr. Vecqueray.

The correspondence, however, relative to Westfeld's case *must* be published. A great wrong has been done. It is the interest alike of Westfeldt and the Public that it should be fully explained and made known: I think it is the interest of Rugby School also; but if (as you say) it is not, then the interests of the School are at variance with those of the Pupils and the Public; and in that case the sooner things are altered the better.

Dr. Hayman's letters state that *you* removed Westfeldt from the School: so it is he that brings your name into the correspondence—not I. If his statements remain uncontradicted, the wrong would appear to lie mainly at your door. If you require Dr. Hayman's consent to the publication of your letter of 21st March, I think you had better ask him for it.

Your name cannot be omitted, and if I do not by next Tuesday receive your consent to publish your first letter, I shall be obliged in the correspondence to assert positively that you were not authorised to remove Westfeldt, that though Dr. Hayman pressed you several times to remove him, you as often declined and you never did remove him, that I received a letter from you on the subject dated 21st March, and in reply to my application for permission to publish that letter, you wrote me your last—in fact, I shall publish your last letter and this.

I regret very much you should be annoyed by having your name mixed up in this affair. I am sure you will see I have a duty to perform to Mr. Westfeldt, and that I was bound to require you to state whether you had (as Dr. Hayman alleged) removed his son or not, and that I am fully justified in publishing your answer.

I remain, dear sir,
Your faithful servant,
J. Vecqueray, Esq.,   A. S. FIELD.
Hill Brow, Rugby.

Hill Brow, Rugby, May 22nd, 1871.

Dear Sir,

22nd May, 1871. Mr. Vecqueray to Mr. Field.

I laid before Dr. Hayman the letter I received from you the day before yesterday, in doing which I feel that I am not taking an undue liberty, since you state in it, that you intend it for publication.

Under the same cover I sent Dr. Hayman a copy of my original letter to you, dated March 21st.

I regret that you are still resolved to publish the correspondence relative to Westfeldt. For my part, I have nothing to add to my communication of last Monday.

Believe me, dear Sir,
Yours faithfully,
A. S. Field, Esq.   J. W. VECQUERAY.

Printed by Libri Plureos GmbH in Hamburg, Germany